KNOCKED 4 SIX!

Going From Hopeless To Hopeful

ORE OGUNGBAYI

Contents

Introduction   vii

1. The Early Years   1
2. Knocked 4 Six!   5
3. My Mother's Version   10
4. January 1973 - October 1984   27
5. Coming Home   36
6. Mirror! Mirror!   41
7. Confidence: An Inside Job   45
8. Mental Health: Let's Have T.E.A!   52
9. Communication: An Outside Job   60
10. A Dozen Lessons   73

Some Thoughts from the Heart   79

I'd like to dedicate this book to:

*My mother, **Victoria**, who contributed to this book and who's always encouraged and supported me through everything in my life.*

*My late husband, **Tunde**, who always went the extra mile for me, and to*

*My two beautiful daughters, **Feyi** and **Feto**, who've kept me going through some very tumultuous times in my life.*

*I'd also like to thank and recognise the **Speakers Trust**, an organisation with whom I've been associated for over 15 years, for their permission to use content (Chapter 9) inspired by their work.*
*A special acknowledgement goes to **Sarah Steed** who was a second pair of eyes at the latter stage of the book and who assisted with the final polish.*

Endorsement

Knocked 4 Six! is the true-life story of Ore Ogungbayi.

When I first began reading Ore's book, I thought I was reading a mystery novel.

I was intrigued, captivated, and frightened by her incredible story, which pieces she then pulled together to give some relief. Ore has taken lessons learned from her life experiences and turned them into practical takeaways and tools for the reader. I highly recommend this book and Ore's Thrive Model.

Are you ready for some suspense? Read this book.

David M.R. Covey, owner & CEO of SMCOVEY and author of the bestselling book,
Trap Tales: Outsmarting the 7 Hidden Obstacles to Success

Introduction

This book has been a long time coming.

Why? Well, you're right to ask...

And I don't really have an answer to that - but then this book is based on actual events, which have been marinating in deep feelings over many years.

Something very unusual happened to me when I was a child and it's impacted every aspect of my life since. I had to feel ready to write it. I needed to feel right about writing it.

Now is the time: I feel right and I feel ready.

My intention is to create a novel-style feel to this book (even though it isn't fiction) and most importantly, that you take away something valuable from my story.

I hope that you can learn from my experiences.

KNOCKED 4 SIX! (Going from Hopeless to Hopeful) is a book designed to entertain, uplift and educate each of you.

My aims are that it's entertaining - in the sense that it's an easy read and feels mostly like a novel - that it's uplifting - in the sense that it inspires hope (and each reader can see that there's always a way forward or a way out) - and that it's educational - in the sense that you'll either learn from some of my experiences or relate to them and then incorporate some of the tools and tips outlined in the latter part into your own life.

My hope is to uplift, enlighten and encourage. And 'hope', as you'll learn over the course of the following chapters, is something that's available to us all.

And now: it's time to tell my story!

I hope you enjoy reading it.

1

The Early Years

In 1965, Stephen and Victoria - a young married couple in their twenties - arrived in London from Nigeria to start a new life together. Their intention was to study in London and then, once they'd successfully achieved their qualifications they would return to Nigeria to raise a family and live happily ever after. The fairy tale ending!

Life in England took them a little by surprise when it became evident that the Nigerian government bursary they'd be relying on wouldn't be enough to live on and that they'd need to work in order to sustain themselves. They weren't work-shy: they set to it right away. Stephen studied electrical engineering and Victoria studied fashion design at the London School of Fashion and they both worked while they studied. Everything seemed to be going according to plan (even though they'd adjusted their plans a bit to accommodate being in employment as well as studying) but then a new situation presented itself: Victoria became pregnant. So far they'd adjusted well to their circumstances but this introduced a whole new dimension to their plans - and a very permanent dimension at that! What were they going to do?

Well, the first thing they did was to accept the situation. And they did this with joy - but joy alone wasn't going to resolve the impracticalities of their new predicament. They really wanted their baby - but, with all the will in the world, there was no way that both Stephen and Victoria could study and work full-time as well as looking after a baby.

On the 18th of February 1966, Victoria gave birth to a beautiful bouncing baby girl in Greenwich, London. They named her 'Ore'.

———

I WAS BORN to parents who loved me but just couldn't look after me at that point in time. Eventually, they came to a decision. It wasn't an easy one but it was the best they could have done under those circumstances: they went to an agency and placed me with foster parents.

I was three months old when I was first placed in the arms of my foster parents, Jock and Raine.

It was love at first sight for Jock and Raine as they welcomed me into their home and life as their daughter. They weren't able to have children of their own and I was an answer to their prayers (although they weren't religious). Despite their atheism they sent me to Sunday school every week.

My life as a little girl was a beautiful one. We lived in Maidstone in Kent and, growing up, I had the life that every child deserves: I was loved and adored by my foster mum and dad, visited regularly by my biological parents (Stephen and Victoria) and I was well integrated with the community and at my school. At such a young age I didn't understand my circumstances. I thought that my foster parents were my real parents and that my biological parents were relatives who cared a lot for me. Considering I was with my foster parents for almost seven years, it's not surprising that I would assume that. I guess one give-away may have been the fact that they were white and I was black - but, as a little girl, I didn't understand the concept of colour or genetics. I only understood the concept of love. And I was definitely loved.

I remember a time when an older friend of mine tried to explain to me where babies came from (and I was intrigued to know!). I was five years old at the time; she must have been around nine. To me, she seemed old and wise and I thought for sure that she knew. So, I registered my interest and she shared her knowledge with me. She said that women have babies when they go to the toilet to do a number two (or, in other words: to move their bowels). I was absolutely horrified by this graphic and scary declaration and immediately wished I hadn't shown interest in gaining some insight into the miracle of birth. Nevertheless, I'd heard it now and I couldn't unhear it. So, as a five-year-old, I decided to take control of my situation: I would never go to the toilet to do a number two *ever again*. I felt fortunate that I hadn't yet had a baby - although I hasten to add that it wasn't that I didn't actually want one (considering how many dolls I had). It was just that I couldn't bear the thought of going through such a scary experience to have one.

When I returned home from school that day I was faced with a bit of a situation: my tummy communicated the message to me that it was time to visit the toilet...

I chose to ignore the warnings and soon developed a bad tummy ache. Full of concern, my foster mum tried to work out what was wrong with me. It wasn't until she was considering calling the doctor that I explained my concerns about accidentally having a baby when I went to the toilet - which I'm sure brought her some relief (and made her laugh). She told me that my friend was wrong and I had nothing to worry about. She encouraged me to use the toilet - but I refused. I wanted reassurance before I took such a huge chance, so I asked her to tell me how we get babies. And she did. She told me something that made so much sense that I wondered how I hadn't already worked it out myself - she said that to have a baby you either go shopping or order one from a catalogue. This made total sense to me because I remembered that we'd gone through a similar process to get my puppy. My puppy was called Peppy and oh, but I loved her! Once my mother had clarified the baby situation to me, I was never going to wonder why my parents were white and why their child was black. I just thought that they liked the colour brown and so had chosen me - the cutest baby they could find.

My school was great and, every single day, I loved attending. It was a fun and safe environment for me and I enjoyed spending time with my friends. I was one of three black children in my school (I mention this for detail, as well as to emphasise a point later in this book). Later in life, my headmistress described me as the brightest student she'd ever taught - and it's clear from that lovely statement that I thrived in that environment. Thriving was always present in my young life as I developed into a bubbly, friendly, kind and confident child. My father, Jock, made me feel that I was the most important thing in the world to him. He told me I was a princess and I believed him because I never wanted for anything - love was there in abundance for me and I was spoilt. A bit spoiled I certainly was, but I wasn't a 'brat' - I never felt that the world owed me anything. However, I did think that anything could be mine if I wanted it and went for it. This confidence and assurance of mine led to me asking a 16-year-old boy to be my boyfriend when I was just six years old. Looking back now, it was a gutsy move (and pretty funny, too).

My daddy had said that I could be anything I wanted to be and that he'd support me in making this happen. I thought that anything was possible, so I decided that I wanted to be a pianist. Sadly, it was never to be: as I write this, I confess that I cannot play a single note.

How did this happen? Where did my dream of being a pianist go?

My dream didn't go anywhere: my circumstances changed suddenly and dramatically, throwing all my childhood hopes and dreams away.

Two months before my seventh birthday, I was abducted.

It changed the course of my life forever.

Knocked 4 Six!

I CAN ONLY TELL this story from the perspective of a child: a child who was six years and 10 months old.

It was December (Christmas time!) - my favourite time of the year. It was 1972, two months from my seventh birthday (my second favourite time of year). My mum, Raine, had taken me to an event in London but my dad had stayed back in Maidstone for a reason I don't remember. The event was a party of some form that I was required to attend because it was put on by some of my African relatives and we'd been invited. I didn't know what the party was in aid of at the time but assumed it was a Christmas party, seeing as it was the festive season and so many parties and events were happening. I was excited to travel to London and be part of a social event.

I remember it was well-attended and everyone had a jolly time eating, drinking and dancing. It was a nice atmosphere and I was just taking it all in, even though I was a little bored because there weren't many children in attendance. So, it was no wonder that I was very pleased when one lady came over to strike up a conversation with me - especially as the conversation revolved around the topic of 'Christmas' and 'presents'. She was speaking my language! I was fully engaged in the conversation, enjoying the opportunity to talk about something I loved and was excited about. I was able to express my excitement about Santa's expected visit on Christmas Eve, my hopes and anticipation for the presents under our tree and the festivities of the day, which I always loved. My boredom disappeared in an instant. Then she told me that she knew about one present I really wanted - a rocking horse! My little face lit up as she mentioned the top item on my list for Santa. Everyone who knew me (and would listen to me) was aware of how badly I wanted this rocking horse: I'd been counting on Santa endorsing me as a 'Good Girl' so that it would be under - or, should I say, next to - the Christmas tree on Christmas Day.

Then she said the words that were to change the course of my life forever: "I've got you the rocking horse - it's downstairs in my car". Those were sweet words to my ears and my reaction probably confirmed how excited I was about this news as she followed with, "would you like to come and take a look?". I was under seven years old, lacking in wisdom and experience, but I did remember my mum telling me never to go off with anyone without her permission, so I asked the lady if she'd asked my mum if it was okay to take me downstairs.

She said yes. I believed her.

At such a tender age, I didn't know that adults lied: I trusted her word and went with her. To this day, I remember asking her this question and I remember being in the lift that took us down to the car park.

When we got to the car park, she explained that the rocking horse was quite bulky and wouldn't fit in her car but there was a lorry around the corner that contained the item and that we'd need to drive there.

So, I got in the car with her.

That was the moment my life changed. I was taken from my mum.

There was no lorry around the corner. I was concerned. The lady reassured me that I had a Christmas present coming that was even more special than the rocking horse (and that my mum was in on it) - the lady said she hadn't wanted to ruin the special surprise and so had used the rocking horse to spark my interest. I insisted on knowing what the surprise was because I was a little concerned about being separated from my mum, even though I thought at the time that it would only be for a short time. She explained that because I'd shown an interest in the past about going on a holiday to the Caribbean and I loved Michael Jackson, both she and my mum had arranged for me to go to a Michael Jackson concert in Barbados for Christmas. I needed a passport to travel, she told me, so my mum had arranged for her to take me for a couple of days to go to the Passport Office in London.

It sounded plausible to me - the idea of being separated from my mum still didn't appeal but the present sounded like such an amazing gift that I thought I should be a brave girl and sacrifice being with my mum for just a few days. I was taken to the Passport Office the next day. Everything happening seemed to be in line with me going to Barbados, so I didn't create a fuss or draw any attention to myself. If I had, it might have prevented me from being taken out of the country and being separated from my parents. Hindsight is a wonderful thing.

For a period of what I would estimate to be two weeks, we were on the run. I didn't know that that was the situation but I remember not sleeping in the same place for more than two or three nights and wearing clothes that didn't belong to me. I remember going on the underground and being scared out of my wits by the frightening sound the trains made and seeing doors open and close by themselves, fearing they'd close on me. Words like Camden and Battersea were constantly being mentioned, and at the time I didn't know what they meant. I now know them to be places in London, so chances are these may have been hide outs during this dramatic episode. I was constantly meeting new people and everywhere we went was busy and so loud. It was all very overwhelming.

It was a scary time but, to me, it seemed worth it for my trip to Barbados to see Michael Jackson. I was due to be reunited with my mum soon anyway.

Finally, following the dramatic events that were my exit from the party, we went to the airport to board the plane that was going to take me to my special Christmas present. I was so excited! At last, the ordeal of being in unfamiliar surroundings with unfamiliar people would come to an end: I'd be reunited with my mum. At the airport I was told that my mum would be meeting us at the airport in Barbados because we weren't flying from the same airport - or, at least, I think that's what I was told. I wouldn't have boarded the plane without making a fuss, otherwise.

Every answer to my questions made sense. So, I went along with the plans. I was a good little girl.

Although I'd never been on a plane before, I had a fear of flying, thanks to a film I'd seen just a few weeks before in which a plane had crashed. I recall asking the air hostess if our plane would crash and remember her reassuring me that it wouldn't. I settled down and looked forward to a happy reunion with my mum and my special Christmas treat.

We arrived the next morning, and I have to say that as I came off the plane I was happy. Before my eyes was a beautiful and sunny place with people buzzing around. It was different to Maidstone. Maidstone was mostly grey and cold: people were calmer and more reserved.

But this new, hot place had an exciting feel to it! I was liking being in Barbados - that is, until I noticed that my mum wasn't at the airport as I'd expected. As you can predict, I asked where she was and was told that her plane would be arriving in a couple of days. I didn't like that answer one bit - but there was nothing I could do about it besides hope that my mum would, as promised, arrive in a couple of days.

I'd been told so many lies by this point but I was none the wiser.

I'd also not yet realised that I wasn't in Barbados. I was across the Atlantic from that Caribbean island, in the coastal state of Lagos. I was in southwestern Nigeria.

There's only so long that the truth can be hidden, even from a naïve six-year-old: sooner or later, it must reveal itself. For me, that realisation would come about a week later.

Finally, I realised that I'd been taken from my family without their knowledge or permission. I realised that I'd never see my mummy and daddy again. I realised that I'd been abducted.

I was only six years old when my whole world came tumbling down around me. I was far from home, I was trapped and I was utterly, completely helpless.

Words cannot express how I felt or how scared I was.

The only thing I can say is...*I was knocked for six.*

My Mother's Version

I WAS NEVER in any danger.

I didn't know this at the time.

A few days after my arrival in Lagos, Nigeria I realised that my mum hadn't arrived – and, at this point, I'd run out of patience, so I did what any six-year-old would do: I had a tantrum!

I wanted my mummy and I wanted her **now**. I no longer wanted the trip or a Michael Jackson concert or anything else. I just wanted my mummy!

For a few days, my abductor and her posse of relatives kept on using delay tactics, saying that she'd be joining me soon. After a couple of days of putting up with my persistent demands, though, they just dropped the bomb on me.

I can remember the words now: "Be quiet! That woman is not your mum – she's your nanny!".

I look back now at that little girl and I can see why some people may wonder if she was stupid or blind as she responded in disbelief and argued bravely that Raine, the English woman, **was** her mum and that they were all liars. At this point, I'd like to remind the reader that I went to my foster parents as a three-month-old baby and had by this time been with them for almost seven years – seven years through which I knew them only as my mum and dad. They'd loved me in a way only a mother and father could and my Scottish dad was my favourite person in the world. He was the first man I ever loved and he was a hero to me.

How could they **not** be my mum and dad? **How** could they not?

And that's when they told me: my abductor was my real mother.

Now, I'd always loved my real mother (although I didn't realise who she really was) because she'd visit often and was always so lovely to me. She had a lovely way about her – and that's why I'd trusted her word and left the party with her. It was because I felt comfortable and safe with her that I was able to bear the separation from my mum and dad. But, in my mind, no matter how nice or lovely she was, she wasn't my real mum. I was not prepared to accept that she was, even though her relatives tried to explain to me that the colour of our skin should be enough to convince me that I was getting my mothers confused.

"Colour of my skin? Is that a thing...?" I'd thought. It was my first exposure to the idea that the colour of your skin matters.

So, was I just stupid or blind? Shouldn't the colour of my skin have given the game away? Well, it didn't! Remember my nine-year-old friend's story about where babies come from and how my mummy had said you go shopping for a baby? As far as I was concerned, that was the way babies got placed in different homes – it had less than nothing to do with skin colour.

Love was what mattered to me. The colour of my mum's or abductor's skin was irrelevant.

Even when I eventually accepted who my abductor was, I couldn't call her "mum". It didn't feel natural to me - it took a while. I was traumatised and I couldn't even voice it. Nobody was listening.

That was one of the biggest battles of my life.

So, what did my biological mum have to say for herself?

At the beginning of this book, I explained the circumstances under which my parents had had to place me with my foster parents. They weren't negligent or selfish parents and it had been clear that they'd both loved and wanted me - but why resort to reclaiming me in this way, so badly hurting the people who'd loved me with all their hearts? And, even worse, in a way that hurt and traumatised the child they claimed to so love? Why not ask to take me back? Why not prepare me for the transition? Surely, this could have been handled better.

When I was old enough and mature enough, I asked my mother for her account of the events: I needed to know why she did what she did.

My own account so far has been based on how these extraordinary events seemed to me, a six-year-old.

Now, I will give you her, adult, account: **my (biological) mother's version!**

MY MOTHER'S VERSION OF EVENTS

On the 29th of March 1965, a very grey and cold morning, my husband and I arrived at Liverpool Harbour on M.V. APAPA - a popular passenger ship from Lagos.

On the 18th of February 1966, I had a beautiful baby girl: Oreoluwa. My husband, Stephen, was so excited! He sprang into action being the perfect father he'd always dreamt of becoming. He looked after me very well and always said that nothing was too much for his two princesses. I was touched by his caring and thoughtful attitude – most Nigerian husbands of that era relied heavily on their wives for financial support but this was one man who believed that if you cannot take care of your family, you don't embark on the journey of marriage. I just happened to be one of the lucky ones.

I couldn't have been happier: but being a first-time mother wasn't easy! There were many challenges and, besides the support I got from my husband during the night and whenever else he was around, I had to do everything the best way I could think of. Having gone through the journey I was now embarking on, some of our friends' wives who came to congratulate us gave me gratefully received advice - but it was still so difficult sometimes for a new mum. The overwhelming love I had for my beautiful daughter, though, made any struggles worthwhile. My husband was the best.

It was the norm among African students studying abroad to put their children into the care of foster parents while they worked and went to school at the same time, so when my daughter was about three months old, we decided to look for a responsible foster mother - although the mere thought of giving my precious daughter to a total stranger brought deep sadness to my heart.

I expressed my concerns to my husband; particularly about my state of mind regarding giving our daughter to a total stranger. Unbeknown to me, he shared my concerns – so we discussed another option. We could take our baby daughter to a daily minder in the morning and pick her up in the evening. We thought about the disadvantages of waking an infant up very early in the morning, taking her to the daily minder during winter, rushing to get to work, rushing back to collect her in the evening... how would this impact our daughter? In the end, after a lot of thought, we decided we didn't want that for Ore. We made up our minds to search extensively for a good foster mother. Many of our friends had been fortunate with their children's foster mothers - although some hadn't been quite so lucky, as a lot of foster mothers just wanted the money they received for being foster parents and would neglect the child the moment their parents' backs were turned.

Two weeks after we started placing adverts in the local newspapers we received two responses: one from a single lady who'd never married and was a former teacher and the other from a couple. Both households were in Kent, so we decided to visit them both. Our first port of call was the former teacher. She was brilliant! She had a very neat house in nice surroundings and she fell in love with our daughter immediately she laid eyes on her. We discussed a couple of things and promised to get back to her as we still had another couple to see. We made our way to the other couple.

When we arrived at the address, our first observation was that the area wasn't bad but the actual house where the couple lived was not as neat as the first we'd visited. They opened the front door in response to our knock and we exchanged introductions before being ushered into their living room and offered coffee, which we gladly accepted. We chatted for about thirty minutes and I knew that our decision would sway in their favour. A quick glance at Stephen told me he was thinking the same as me. I guessed that the wife, Raine, was probably in her early forties and the husband, Jock, maybe early fifties. We were told that they didn't have any children but that Jock had a son with whom he'd lost contact during the war. We discussed our fears around making sure we were giving our daughter to the right people - people who'd look after her like their own. They both assured us that if we trusted them enough to give her to them, we'd never have any cause to regret it. On leaving, we promised to get in touch with them about our decision. We also told them about our visit to the other lady.

On our way back to London, we made the decision to give our daughter to Raine and Jock. We both had a strong feeling that they'd look after her very well - not that we doubted that the first woman would take care of her; we just loved the idea of our daughter living in a home with a father figure. We phoned the couple the following day to let them know that we'd chosen them to look after our daughter. They were so happy! They promised to love her as their own. We didn't know why, but we believed them.

The next weekend, we packed everything that belonged to our daughter and headed to Maidstone, Kent where my precious daughter was handed over to the couple. We agreed on how much we'd be paying them every month and told them we'd visit every two weekends: they told us we could visit anytime we wished without prior notice and, with that statement, I was a hundred per cent sure my daughter would be well cared for. Some of our friends' children's foster mothers would never allow a visit without being previously informed - their reasoning for this was because the child could be in a messy state of appearance at any point and they wanted to make sure that the child appeared clean and well-dressed all the time.

Before we left, four hours later, I called Raine to one side and pleaded with her to keep her promise. She hugged me, telling me not to worry and said that Ore would be well cared for.

Leaving our daughter behind was very traumatic for Stephen and me. As a man, he tried to hide his feelings, but I could see he was as unhappy as I was. We hardly spoke throughout the journey back to London, each engrossed in our own thoughts.

When we arrived back at our room, the place seemed lifeless without the cry of my daughter. That was the point at which I started to cry. I think back and I realise that it was this action of mine that made Stephen bravely put his unhappiness aside. He sat with me on the bed, holding my hand and looking me straight in the eye to say, "you know we told them we'll be coming every two weekends. If for any reason at all we ever feel or think that our child is being neglected in any way, we'll bring her back and you'll have to be a full-time mother. Then, we'll decide on what you can learn before we return to our country - but I'm sure they'll take good care of her". I felt reassured. I wiped my tears and smiled at him, telling him what a wonderful person he was.

That night, I didn't sleep very well – in fact, it took almost a week before I could get hold of myself. We phoned the couple every day. They weren't irritated or angry with our anxiety: they just kept assuring us that they were committed to their promise. Two weeks later, we visited our daughter.

When we saw her, all our fears and anxiety disappeared: she looked very well. Raine and Jock cooked lunch for us all. As we continued chatting at the dinner table after our lunch, it just felt as if we'd known them for years - we were like one big, happy family. Five hours later, our hearts full of joy and gratitude to God for answering our prayers and giving us the type of foster parents we'd asked for, we left. The visit pattern continued. If Stephen was working when we were due to go, I'd take the train.

Our fortnightly visits never stopped.

My daughter was growing fast and her foster parents - particularly Jock - adored her. We had a very good relationship with them. Stephen called Jock "Dad" and he, in return, called him "son"; they were very close. Raine was also very protective of my daughter.

The weekends I visited my daughter were the most important and exciting times of my life. My husband would play music on the way and, seeing our daughter, taking her in her pram and going out for a walk with the foster parents would bring us immense joy. They were happy times – Raine and Jock always cooked lunch and we'd sit at the dining table together to eat and talk about current affairs. We never spent less than five hours there.

My daughter started walking when she was nine months old! The week she started walking, her foster mother phoned to tell us that she had a surprise for us – and, although we tried, we couldn't guess what the surprise could be. It was a very pleasant one to discover: we got out of the car to see our daughter toddling towards us unaided! They said they were waiting for the sound of our car and immediately they heard us they all came out – they'd wanted us to see the surprise they'd mentioned on the phone. We were ecstatic! Her dad scooped Ore up and kissed her chubby cheeks, after which he gave her to me for my own hug. Stephen and Jock were getting closer and closer and our relationship with them grew stronger. It was no surprise when, during our last visit in November of that year, the two men suggested we come and spend Christmas with them while they'd come and spend New Year's with us. The plan was to go up on Christmas Eve and return on Boxing Day - then they'd come down on 31st December and return on New Year's Day.

When we got to their house on Christmas eve the sitting room was illuminated with Christmas tree lights, the house was so warm and cosy and having the opportunity to stay there for three days in a row with our daughter gladdened my heart. Likewise, Stephen couldn't have been happier. We took some presents with us and bought our daughter some beautiful clothes. We bought a thick cardigan for Jock and a beautiful blouse for Raine. We all enjoyed our Christmas lunch of roast turkey, roast potatoes, vegetables and Yorkshire pudding with sauce and was followed by jelly, after which we all sat to watch the television. Boxing Day went quickly and, before we knew it, we were packing our things to go back to London. The only consolation was that we'd be seeing them a couple of days later.

Stephen and I had decided before we went for Christmas to tell them that we'd like our daughter to come to us for occasional weekends - sometimes they could come with her, too. Jock and Raine had agreed to our request.

We invited a couple of our friends to spend New Years' day with us and, with Ore, Raine and Jock, we all ate, drank and danced to different styles of celebratory music, noticing our special guests were thoroughly enjoying themselves and enjoyed getting acquainted with some of our friends. Our friends were envious of our relationship with our daughter's foster parents, who we now regarded as our own family.

Seeing how much they'd enjoyed themselves when they came to London, we asked them the next time we went visiting if they'd like to go on occasion to some of our friends' parties. Raine said yes but Jock said he'd only come sometimes because he didn't particularly like going to parties. And that was the way it was! If it was a wedding, my husband would go and pick them up from the train station and, after the party, he'd take them to a bed and breakfast that he'd have booked in advance and both of us would go back in the morning and take them to the train station.

Our lives continued like this for a while - both of us going to work and school and getting closer to our daughter's foster parents.

We observed that Ore's foster father loved our daughter very dearly and she, in return, was awfully close to him. He spoilt her, always buying things for her whenever he went out.

He suggested to my husband a few times that he'd like us to leave my daughter with them when the time came for us to return to our country, Nigeria. Stephen always said he'd wait and see what the future held. Jock was still extremely close to my husband and our daughter called Jock "Daddy" and my husband, "Daddy Stephen" - she called her foster mother "Mummy" and me "Mummy Vicky". We didn't mind this at all! It was important that she felt secure in her home.

My husband eventually had to leave England and return to Nigeria to set things up for us.

It was such an emotional goodbye: we all went with him to Euston Station, from where he took the train to Liverpool, to return to Nigeria the way we'd come a few years before: by ship. He took our daughter's foster parents aside and promised he'd never forget them. He said that, after he'd settled properly in Nigeria, he'd invite them to come and stay with us for a couple of months.

"We're going to miss you!" they said to him, "Please write as often as possible to let us know how you're faring".

"I will", promised Stephen – and, with those parting words, he hugged them and everyone who went to see him off before coming to me, holding me tightly and saying into my ear, "I am going to miss you terribly".

"I'm missing you already", I replied. I was so sad: I wasn't sure when I'd see him next. As the train started to move away, I burst into tears. The foster parents wore sad faces, too.

I continued with my life as usual, working Monday to Friday and going straight from work to the station to get the train to Kent. I was at peace with the world.

This peace, however, was to be short-lived.

It was shattered by an unfortunate incident involving a misunderstanding with another family member, who had, on our recommendation, also placed their child - a son - in the care of Raine and Jock at the time. These relatives had taken their son to Nigeria for a brief visit, promising to bring him back and return him to Raine and Jock: but, when they'd told their family back home of this plan, their family wouldn't hear of it. So, they'd had to go back on their word to Raine and Jock.

That had hit the caring foster couple extremely hard. It wasn't long before that event had a clear impact on our relationship – in no time at all, the trust was just gone. I'd noticed the change in their attitude towards me and I'd been frightened by it.

Jock and Raine had become moody most of the time, to the point that I started to dread going to them at the weekends. Of course, because I needed to see Ore, I had no choice but to continue as usual.

Over the space of a few weeks, I'd asked twice to take Ore to London for a week because I had my annual leave. They'd refused. They said that I should come and spend my leave with them. I was never allowed to be alone with Ore anymore and my heart was breaking into smithereens.

Although I'd tried to hide their latest actions from Stephen in Nigeria, it was at this point that I had no choice but to tell my husband. He wrote to them about my allegations right away – but, far from giving him any cogent reason for their behaviour, they'd played down the whole situation.

Three months after all this started, I was in Jock and Raine's house in Maidstone on a weekend visit. With relations cooler than ever before, I picked up that Sunday's *News of the* World and started reading. Scanning through, I saw the word "adoption" – the piece caught my eye and I read it all the way through.

It was about a new law the UK government had enacted that could allow a foster parent to adopt any child who'd been in their care for six years or more.

My jaw dropped. Ore was six. She'd been with her foster parents since was just three months old.

It was clear that Jock and Raine had also read the piece.

Neither of us made any comment - but I could see the joy in their faces, like a horrifying reverse reflection of my own feelings: I was dying inside.

I pretended not to be bothered with the story.

Back in London on my lunch break that Monday, I dashed to the Post Office to send a telegram to Stephen intimating him about the new law: "They will take my daughter away from me," I wrote. Stephen replied immediately, reassuring me that we'd find a way to resolve it. But that wasn't much of a consolation to me. **How** were we to resolve it? I didn't know.

The next month was a waking nightmare: there's no other way to describe it. Any love that had existed between Ore's biological parents and her foster carers was disappearing at an alarming rate. I'd already lost over a stone in weight from worrying: I just couldn't eat. At night, all I could think about was how I could prevent our daughter from being taken away from us.

When Ore's foster parents started behaving in an even stranger manner towards me, I confided my predicament to my work friend, who was also from Nigeria. From that moment on, whenever we were on lunch, all we discussed was how I could get Ore back. We thought that if I could get the chance to take her, I would take her to Germany first and from there, we could go to Nigeria - but we both knew that this would be impossible because Ore was never allowed out of Jock and Raine's sight now when I visited.

My uncle-in-law was worried about the effect the whole episode was having on me, so he wrote to Stephen telling him about his concern for my health. I was losing weight drastically from a lack of sleep and loss of appetite, but neither he nor Stephen could come up with any solution. Stephen was terribly afraid that I might become depressed, so he wrote to Jock and Raine to tell them (beg them really) to continue to be the family they had been to him since the first day we met them. He also asked them whether, during the time they'd known him, they'd ever found him wanting either through his relationship with them or his dealings with others. All he needed from them was their understanding.

It all fell on deaf ears and it was then that I really acknowledged: they knew they were holding the ace card.

I had to act fast. I came up with a plan.

At work the next day, I told my friend what I planned to do. She hugged me, saying I was a genius. "If that plan doesn't work," she said, "nothing else will". I sent a telegram to Stephen informing him about what I planned to do. His telegram reply was swift: he agreed. As much as he hated to hurt Jock and Raine in any way, they'd disappointed him more than he could ever have envisaged – and, because of this, he said, we must do everything possible to get Ore back. He only wished that he could be in England to support me. He promised to write to all his friends and even his uncle and ask them to support me in any way they could.

He told his uncle first, who was impressed with my plans. As he told each of his friends, they all promised to support me in whatever way I needed. Funnily enough, everyone who heard about my plans asked me how in heavens' name I ever come up with it. Well, I told them all: when you're a mother about to lose your child to another woman, there is **nothing** you won't do to keep hold of your baby. I'd already told Stephen in one of my letters that I wouldn't come to Nigeria if it was to be without Ore.

The first part of my plan was to tell my daughter's foster parents that my uncle (my father's younger brother) had recently died in Nigeria (he'd actually died two years before we came to England). I explained this to them and then politely let them know that Nigerian custom dictates that my child or children (in particular, my firstborn) must attend the funeral ceremony. I must throw him a farewell party in London, I told them, on the same day they were to hold the funeral in Nigeria. My dead uncle's daughter lived in London and the party was to be held in her apartment, with her own children also coming from their foster parents: we had to make the party look as real as possible.

I was a bit apprehensive that they might not show up - but they did, and it was the most wonderful feeling when Raine and Ore arrived at my cousin's house. I went to the toilet and wept for joy. I'd never been a callous person but with Jock and Raine's odd behaviour and increasing emotional distance eroding the trust in our relationship over the past several months, I was at breaking point. I'd been driven to act against my nature. I've never been an ingrate by any standard and neither had Stephen - but where one's child is concerned, I'm sure that most parents would agree that they'd do anything and everything not to lose their children: not even to their own mother.

There were approximately twenty-five people at the event, with much eating, drinking and dancing. In time Ore's foster mum put her to bed. We'd made sure beforehand that the bedroom they were to use was obscured from the sitting room where the festivities would be taking place. An hour after the party had begun, I received a phone call.

This was stage two: it was my husband's friend on the line, calling to tell me it was time for us to make our move. As Raine had been checking Ore every half an hour, we waited for her to check again. When she'd returned to the living room, I made a dash for it with Ore. It was the strangest feeling: Ore kept asking, "where are you taking me?" and I told her we were going to pick up the rocking horse I'd got her for Christmas. "But where is my mummy?", she asked – that was even stranger to hear. I assured her not to worry: her mummy would soon join us. She kept quiet after that.

Ten minutes after we got to Stephen's friend's house, his phone rang and we were told that all hell had broken loose. Immediately Raine had found out about the disappearance, she'd started crying uncontrollably, threatening to kill herself. She'd then held my uncle-in-law to ransom, demanding that he take her to my house otherwise she would make good on her threat. She was so convincing to the point where all the knives on the premises had to be hidden and he agreed to her demands. On reaching my place, she was told I wasn't home. Unbeknown to her, I had actually already vacated that premises and was staying with Stephen's friend. Raine now made Stephen's uncle take her to his own apartment: but, when they got there, she saw that I wasn't there, either. Raine didn't believe that my uncle-in-law (who I referred to as "Uncle D") was unaware of my plans: she threatened to kill herself again and it was at that point (he later told me) that he'd advised her to file a report at the police station. Uncle D took her to the nearest police station to make the report and he later told us that it was as she was being questioned by the police that they realised it was the biological mother of the child who was responsible for the abduction.

Raine was then told that, because it was the biological mother who'd taken Ore - and Jock and Raine hadn't legally adopted her - there was nothing the police could do. They advised her that, if she wished, she could take civil action against me. We were told that she blasted the policemen on duty for not doing their jobs properly, demanding to know whether they were aware of the new law regarding fostered children: but, eventually, she agreed to go back to Uncle D's house for the night. Uncle D told me that he'd had to hide all the knives in the house in case she tried to make good on her suicide threats. Raine had called Jock to tell him what had happened: he was enraged. Speaking next to Uncle D, Jock proceeded to tell him that I was wasting my time because he'd make sure I never took Ore to Nigeria. Uncle D promised Jock he'd try his best to find us and talk me into returning Ore to them.

When Uncle D was taking Raine to the station the next morning, she told him I'd never get my daughter out of the country. Both she and her husband, she said, would alert all the airports and all the harbours in the country: if I tried to leave with Ore, I'd be arrested for child abduction.

Hearing Uncle D relay that to me, my heart sank into my shoes. Was I back to square one already? I had no way of knowing how far my daughter's foster carers would go to carry out their threats – and it started to impact me, again.

Three days later, I was advised to leave our hiding place - I needed to get Ore vaccinated before we travelled. I wondered whether Jock and Raine would have given my name to the London hospitals, too: would the staff know who we were the moment we walked through the clinic doors? Not knowing how far they would go, I was terrified. For weeks, my daughter and I were constantly on the move, shifting from one place to the next: we were, literally, on the run.

I remember that we once managed to settle for several days in one place, with a friend of Stephen's – it was such a relief. But before long at all, we had to leave there, too: because my husband's friend started to tell me to give Ore back to her foster parents. He told me that he felt they would continue to take good care of her. When I told Uncle D about this, he told me to get out of there right away and not say

24

where we were going, in case he decided to tell them our whereabouts.

So, once again, we were on the run – and, this time, we were on the run from some of our own friends, too.

Once Uncle D had relayed to me the continued threats from Ore's foster carers, he told me to phone them and tell them the reason I'd taken her. He said I should tell them that it was because of the way they'd prevented me from spending time alone with my daughter and that I'd bring her home the following week. I did as he suggested and made the call. A week later, Stephen sent them a telegram from Nigeria telling them how deeply sorry he was to have hurt them and that Ore and I were already safely back in Nigeria. He thanked them for all they'd done for us but made sure to make them realise that things would have worked out differently if they'd only trusted him. He still assured them that he would keep his promise if they still wanted to remain friends with us.

Stephen lied to Jock and Raine: he told them that Ore and I were already in Nigeria. He didn't feel good about it but saw no other option - he needed to get them off my back so that I'd be able to get Ore the vaccinations she needed without having to look over my shoulders each time I went out. It was a good move: after this, the threats stopped and my mind was finally at rest.

On the very last day of that year - 1972 – Ore and I boarded a British Caledonian aircraft. When the plane was airborne I silently sang a song of praise to God for being with me and making it possible for me to go home with Ore.

A lot of members of our family came to welcome us home (in fact, there were so many that they'd hired a bus to fit them all in!) and they thanked me for making sure that I came home with my child.

It was like a hero's welcome.

Although I counted it as a huge achievement that I'd been able to bring my daughter back home safely, I couldn't help but feel sorry for the foster parents. They were so unhappy.

Over the next few years, Stephen would keep in constant touch with them. When Ore had reached her final year of primary school, she could speak our language and knew about our culture and customs - so we'd made up our minds to speak to her foster parents and look for a good secondary school for Ore near Maidstone. We'd be bringing her back to England as soon as she finished primary school in Nigeria. Raine still found it difficult to forgive us, but Stephen told me not to worry - he felt that, once they'd seen that we'd make good on our promise, she'd come around.

But that just wasn't to be: two months later, my Stephen died in a ghastly motor accident. He was 38 and I was 31.

The plan to send Ore back to England to continue her education just couldn't happen. I wanted her by my side.

> 4
>
> # January 1973 - October 1984

THE FIRST TIME I heard the <u>full</u> account of what had happened all those years ago was when I started writing this book. I must admit that it was quite an emotional experience for me: my heart broke for my birth mother, and the years of resentment I'd felt towards her for having taken me from my lovely and loving family then turned into understanding and appreciation for a mother who loved her child with every fibre of her being. I expressed my love for her and my sadness at the harrowing experience she'd endured at such a young age.

She'd left England with me on the 31st of December 1972 and we arrived in Nigeria on the 1st of January 1973. New Year's Day... talk about a new beginning!

Nigeria was to become my home for the next 11 years and, unbeknown to me when I first arrived, I was in for a particularly challenging time.

Realising that I'd been literally kidnapped and that the chances of me returning home and seeing my mummy and daddy again were very slim was a huge shock for six-year-old me. But I held on to the hope that my mummy and daddy loved me so much that they'd soon come and get me.

They never did.

I felt let down by all the adults in my life. For the first time in my young life, I felt alone. What was I to do? I was scared and helpless. There was no way I was going to call the woman who abducted me "mummy", no matter how many adults constantly told me she was my mother. It didn't feel natural to me at all and it took quite some time before I could manage it. The word "mummy" just struggled to come out of my mouth: it seemed to get stuck in my throat. Over the next decade, that was only the first of many hurdles I'd have to figure out how to jump. This little girl - "me" - would have to learn a whole new way of living - she'd have to fit into a new family and learn who everyone was, fit into a new place where nothing was familiar, learn a new language, start in a new school, acquire a taste for new and spicy food, get accustomed to the heat and make new friends.

Friends! This is where I decided to start - it was the most appealing of all the prospects available to me at the time. I was a friendly, bubbly, confident little girl, which is why everyone in Maidstone seemed to love me. Imagine my shock and upset when I encountered rejection and name-calling in my attempts to integrate. Names like Roly Poly, Elephant, Fatso, Kutelu and Okotombo - each meaning 'fat' - became names I was commonly referred to. I'd never been called fat in my life and I'd never been treated so poorly either. It really hurt. I was already extremely vulnerable and unhappy. This just compounded my sense of loss.

In Maidstone, as mentioned earlier, I was one of three black children in my school and yet it never held any meaning for me but here I was in Nigeria, "with my people", and for the first time in my life I felt different.

To put it simply: this is what started my journey down the road to self-hate and a loss of self-confidence. I got called names at school, at home by some of our relatives and even on the streets when running errands. By the time I started secondary school, I'd got the message that I was a social outcast and not good enough for most things or most people.

I was a bright child and still did well at school (even in this unfamiliar landscape), which made me a little popular - but only during exam time when others could sneak a peek at my answers to further their chances of passing. Apparently, I was worth knowing **then** - and only then - but what was really happening?

I was being used by people because I was desperate to be liked. That's what was happening. I so badly wanted to be accepted and approved of but my self-esteem was, by that point, rock-bottom and the way I presented myself was, frankly, begging to be made a target and be taken advantage of. People would say unkind things to me and call me names without caring about my feelings and without any fear of any consequences - because they knew there wouldn't **be** any consequences. And what could I do? Nothing! I longed for my English home and I resented my mum (even though I really had grown to love her dearly) for taking me and then bringing me to a place where I didn't belong, didn't fit in and wasn't accepted.

I could never identify as a Nigerian because, to me, I'd lost my identity. Everything I'd once considered to be true now wasn't true. I was in a place that was supposed to be my "roots" and yet I was being marginalised and made to feel worthless and, despite learning the language and their ways, I always identified as an English girl (in my mind), because it was in England that I'd lived freely and happily as a child and it was in England that I'd been accepted for everything I was and everything I wasn't. I longed for England!

As a child, I made up so many stories about why this had happened to me and, as I got older (and as more upsetting things happened), I just concluded that I was unlucky. Whenever anything bad happened or if things didn't go my way, I'd say to myself: "why do bad things always happen to me?". Growing up, I felt hard done by and nurtured no hope of any improvement in my situation. I was even called "Blacky" by the locals because I tanned easily. All my time in Nigeria had made me darker in complexion - which, according to some fellow Nigerians, was another reason to call me names and ridicule me. I was frequently described as the "Black Fat Girl" ("black" here meaning "darker than others").

When I first arrived in Nigeria, though, I did manage to make one friend, who became very dear to me. It happened a few months after my unexpected arrival, following a move from my uncle's home where we'd been staying temporarily until our own accommodation was ready. At this point, I should add that my uncle was a very lovely man who did his best to make me feel welcome. My mum and dad also provided a lovely and loving home for me.

My new friend, Tayo (who I'll refer to as "TG") was my neighbour; she lived in the flat next to ours. She'd also been born in England and moved to Nigeria with her family - something that we had in common, albeit with drastically different relocation stories. She was just two months older than me but seemed so much more mature! And that's something that benefited me: she took me under her wing and started to integrate me into our community in her little way. I loved her and I needed her and she was with me all the way. Although we attended different primary schools, as soon as it came time to progress to secondary school, I desperately wanted to join her at Marywood Grammar School - she was already there because she was a year ahead of me. Thankfully, I got my wish and was able to go to the same secondary school as TG! She introduced me to her friends and just that alone made the transition so much easier for me. I was known as her 'little sister' and was treated with more respect than usual because of it.

TG was popular, attractive and slim: everything that I wanted to be but wasn't. It never occurred to me at the time that I was defining and qualifying others and myself using the wrong measuring tools, but I was young (worse, actually: I was a teenager!). I was clearly naïve and also lacked a real understanding: thankfully, I know better now.

As well as being physically attractive, TG also had wonderful inner qualities (you know, those qualities that **actually** define a person, rather than how their face, skin or body appear) - she was kind to me and a lot of fun to have around, never once put me down and always made me feel that I was important to her. This mattered to me. A lot. I will always be grateful to her for loving me for who I was.

A few years into my secondary school life, TG and her family moved away. She had to change schools. This was obviously upsetting for me but, thankfully, not devastating - because she'd played her role well and I already felt at home in school. I was finally doing ok! That isn't to say that I still didn't have experiences with name-calling and put-downs but I was accustomed now to being one of the underdogs and I'd accepted that I'd never be popular, admired or "cool" (whatever that means). My strategy for life was to do well at school, go to university and build an amazing career so that people would respect me for what I'd achieved. I'd picked up that this was The Nigerian Way: be successful and have money, then no one would disrespect you. A bit of a sad state of affairs... but at least it offered me some hope of one day being accepted and respected. I was going to be okay. I was going to **survive**!

Sometime after TG moved (and I cannot remember if it was her 15th or 16th birthday), she invited me to her home for her birthday party. In fact, I think it was her 15th birthday because I can recall that I was living at my Grandma's place at the time and remember being 14 years old - just a couple of months behind TG in age.

It hadn't been in my parents' plan for me, either, that we'd be living at my Grandma's, but as you'll recall from my mother's story, my dad had died in a horrific car accident a few years before (when I was 11). This tragedy had led to my mother and our family falling on very hard times. We'd had to leave our family home.

My father had been quite a successful young man and, to me, our lives had seemed great. He was the manager of the top musician of the time (King Sunny Ade!), who was rivalled only by Ebenezer Obey. It was an interesting lifestyle, being in the company of celebrities often and with my father in the limelight - there were lots of comings and goings in our home. Life was buzzing - it seemed good from where I was standing. It only ever occurred to me much later in life that I never milked or took advantage of the situation to boost my ever-failing profile. It'd never even occurred to me! Those who knew of my struggles knew - those who didn't...didn't. End of!

The death of my father had come as a huge and awful shock. It changed our lives in so many ways. Feyi Akinrujomu, fondly known as Stephen in England, was a good father and husband and he really made our world bright. It was a blow to lose him - another knock in my young life.

Why do bad things always happen to me? That was the question on my mind yet again.

Some time after his death, some older members of his family came from his hometown in Ondo - and took everything that belonged to him (us) including his car, clothes and TV. We were left with nothing. My mother was only 31 years old at the time and she now had four children with her (the youngest just five months old). How cruel and greedy can people be?! Our situation became so dire that we had to leave our home and move in with my mum's mother for a while. I couldn't help but ask why bad things always happened to me.

It was while we were living at my Grandma's that TG invited me to her birthday party. I was so excited to be invited! She was cool and popular and nobody had ever invited me to their party before (well - just family members) because I was not seen as cool - or even accept-able. And, once again, TG showed me that I mattered to her. I remember that day well, even down to the ugly maxi dress that my mum had insisted on buying for me. She had made a sacrifice to afford it, so I had no choice but to wear it.

I was dressed up as a nine-year-old going to a teenager's party and, even though I knew that I didn't look the part, it didn't matter to me because I'd never considered myself attractive or cool anyway. So it just wasn't really an issue. It took me two hours and three buses to get to the party and I was excited the whole way there! When I got to my destination, I walked happily to her door, so looking forward to seeing her and partying with her. The idea of hanging out with her cool crowd filled me with glee - I could barely contain my excitement!

When I got to the front door, I was accosted by two boys who demanded to know what I wanted. This understandably took me by surprise: I was thrown off my guard. I wasn't expecting that at all, especially as I knew TG very well and she'd personally requested my presence - so I did the polite thing and responded to their question by telling them that TG had invited me.

Both of them looked me up and down, analysing and assessing me. When they made eye contact with me again their faces were filled with disgust and disapproval. Then they asked me if I was sure. Was I sure that TG had invited me? My heart started pounding fast and my tummy knotted as I sensed something bad was about to happen to me again but I held myself together and asked if they would kindly go and get my friend so that she could confirm that I was there on her invitation. People were watching all this but nobody intervened to spare me the humiliation; instead, I heard a few quiet giggles. I was close to tears. I felt so bad and worthless but I knew that once TG came to the door I'd be vindicated and those two rude boys would be put in their place.

They returned to the front door a few moments later, empty-handed, and said they couldn't find her. I was **gutted**! There was no way for me to communicate with her (back then, we didn't have mobile phones), so I was helpless. I was defeated. The boys didn't let me in and I had to turn around in front of everyone watching and leave.

Two hours and three buses… I cried all the way home. I had a lot of time to think about this latest humiliation of mine on this long journey and I concluded: "Ore, you are nothing! You are worthless!".

The last trace of the bubbly, friendly, confident little girl from Maidstone had gone. This was one of the biggest knocks of my life. How could I come back from this?

TG never knew that I turned up at her party - until I told her in 2020, after reconnecting with her during the first UK lockdown. She was shocked and horrified and, to my delight and vindication, said she'd have given them a piece of her mind and put them in their place if she'd known. She reminded me how important I'd always been to her and - even after 40 years - it brought tears to my eyes to hear that from my dear friend.

My life in Nigeria and as a young person continued along these lines. I can't go into every incident or experience in this book because my intention is to keep it as short as possible so that anyone can read it without having to give up too much of their time.

My aim is to share a summary of myself (as a young person) and my story with whoever reads this and provide a source of hope to everyone. Life is full of knocks: we all experience them. They're not just reserved for me, so I don't want this to feel like I've had it harder than others (because I definitely haven't!) but the knocks I've experienced, just like the knocks you've experienced in your life, are unique to each of us. My hope is for you and anyone else who reads this to see that our knocks are sometimes our building blocks in life to something bigger or better - or sometimes they're to teach us humility and empathy for others and sometimes they're just there simply to make life difficult.

Well, if they exist simply to make life difficult, I can tell you from experience: our responsibility is to overcome them and learn something.

I was **stuck** in Nigeria for 11 years. I must say that I'd not be the person I am today without the Nigerian experience. Now, I can say that I'm grateful for my Nigerian experience - the language, the people, the culture, the food and, so importantly, the friendships that I now have.

In October 1984, after years of longing, I returned to England. I returned to the land of my birth.

The six-hour flight seemed to take forever. I just couldn't wait.

5

Coming Home

I wish I could say that returning home was all I'd dreamt it would be.

My mother brought me back to England - to London, where she'd travelled with my father all those years ago. Once again, I had to adjust to a completely new place because London was nothing like Maidstone and I hadn't returned to my English mum and dad. I didn't know where they were - and I didn't dare ask my mum. She'd told me once when I was a child that they'd moved. For my first task in England, all I wanted was to find them - but how was I going to do that?

In the meantime, I was not finding being back in England to be what I'd expected. I was experiencing a lot of put-downs, just like I did in Nigeria, with those around me making me feel small about my acquired Nigerian accent, my dress sense and my weight. Those people were mostly Nigerians (just now in a different location) and I had to wonder: why? What was it about me that was unacceptable? Why were they constantly putting me down? In Nigeria, I was always being told that "these are your people" but that certainly didn't feel true to me. I never felt that I belonged there when I was in Nigeria and now, back in England, it was just the same.

I was frightened by the thought of being the underdog once again but I was at a complete loss as to how to claim back my power. I wanted to belong and I tried so hard to fit in. At 18 years old, acceptance and a sense of belonging were probably the most important things to me (besides my education, that is. I was still an excellent student and I loved school).

It was tough, trying to feel accepted in England. Believe it or not, at one point I was having such a tough time that I actually wanted to return to Nigeria! At least there, I thought, I had worked out a coping strategy and managed to have a life that I could bear. The last thing I expected in England was to feel lost, to feel like an outsider and to feel worthless. That was not the England I remembered. It was not the England I'd longed for.

I enrolled in college for my 'A' Levels and started to carve out a life of some sort for myself. I had to live in several different places before I could eventually settle in properly - Camberwell, Tottenham, Westbourne Grove, Pimlico and, finally, Brixton, where I lived for 11 years.

The years between me returning to England and finally 'finding myself' were trying - but I learnt a lot along the way about myself and about others. I grew from a dejected 'doormat' into a human being who I personally loved and respected highly. The journey through those years was strewn with rejection, betrayal, financial hardship, self-loathing, low self-esteem, low confidence and a deep sense of worthlessness. But it also included friendship, loyalty, support, love and growth. I learnt something so important: that, no matter how bad things might seem or how people might behave towards you, there are always good things and good people (like TG) who will bear you up because they see and can appreciate the **real** you.

I was able to bear a lot of unpleasant behaviour towards me because of the love of my family and some good friends I was fortunate to have. They all constantly reminded me of my qualities and attributes and they saw me as a beautiful being, despite (I thought) how I looked.

My weight was such an issue for me - I really felt that everyone judged me purely on that. All those years ago, it had so quickly got to a point where **I** judged **myself** purely on my body's weight.

And that's what the real problem was: I'd allowed years of abuse to define who I thought that I was. There was no glimpse of the happy, confident, bubbly six-year-old me who'd asked that sixteen-year-old boy to be my boyfriend. There was nothing left of the 'me' who was free.

It was two years after returning to England that I was reunited with my foster parents and, in the end, it wasn't something I'd planned: good fortune had somehow been accorded me. I had made some attempts to find my foster parents but, really, they'd been feeble attempts. I was so young when I was separated from them and I was still new to being back in England: those first couple of years, I was ill-equipped to get results.

My reunion with them came about as a result of my mum needing to re-instate her residency in the UK following her long absence. In order to accomplish this, her solicitors had advised her to go to my Primary School in Maidstone (Brunswick House) to obtain evidence that I'd been a pupil there. This was to substantiate her claim that her children were born in England. In order to achieve this, she needed me to go to the school with her - which I did happily because this would be my first time back in Maidstone! Because I'd been told that my foster parents had moved when I was little, it had never occurred to me to go back to Maidstone to look for them. On this wonderful day, we met with the lovely headteacher, who remembered me well, and we obtained the evidence my mum needed. It was so special to me just to be back there.

On our way out, I realised that I remembered where I'd lived as a child and (even better!) that I could recall how to make my way there. I told my mum that I'd like to pop 'round there to ask the new occupants if they happened to have a forwarding address. My mum was okay with this but said that I should go alone. So I did.

As I approached the house, all kinds of warm memories came rushing back to me. Oh, I so wanted to see Jock and Raine again! So, imagine my surprise (shock, actually) when I knocked tentatively on the door... to find it opened by Jock. I was stunned. He was stunned. I was not prepared for this as a possible outcome. My Mummy and Daddy had been here all along. I couldn't believe it.

I felt so robbed.

He invited me in - and I accepted with no thought for my mum, who was still waiting for me. At that moment, I was so overcome with emotions... if I had seven lifetimes, I just couldn't describe them all to you. There were so many thoughts rushing through my mind that I forgot that mum was waiting for me.

A lot of things were explained to me on that day by him and, consequently, by my biological mother: things were put into some kind of perspective for me. I visited with my dad for an hour and promised to come back when my mum, Raine, was in.

All the way back to London that day, I cried and cried as I thought about the pain they'd endured and the fear that my biological mother must have experienced because of **love**. The love for a child that they all wanted.

This was the day that my healing process started. That was the day I realised how valuable and important I was. On the train journey home, I recalled that the headteacher had told my mum that the reason she remembered me was because I'd been the brightest child she'd ever taught.

A lot of messages came through to me that day - and they became clearer still over time. All four of my parents' love for me was so strong, and the headteacher whom I had so admired as a child admired me right back! There must have been something admirable and loveable about me, then. These were powerful messages for a young person with absolutely no self-worth to hear and, in time, they'd come to form a crucial piece of the me I gradually came to love.

After this reunion, I continued to visit and stay with my foster parents and we were able to rebuild a wonderful relationship that bridged the gap of those lost years. I loved them still and they loved me! They'd kept so many photographs of me, along with my baby book and the two pretty little dresses I wore on my first birthday.

Many years later, my eldest child, Feyi, took her first steps in Jock and Raine's home too, and both she and my second daughter, Feto, wore those same two dresses for photographs on their first birthdays.

Yes, I went on to marry a wonderful man (another story for another time) and together we had two wonderful daughters. And that was something that, since that horrible day when I was turned away from my friend's birthday party at 14, I'd assumed would never happen for me.

It just goes to show.

Over the years since returning to England, I've learnt to re-connect with my true self and appreciate myself for everything I am and everything I am not. Being the 'perfect human being' (something we all want to some degree) was not something that was on offer to me: in fact, it's not available to anyone. The grass is not always greener on the other side and every human being has "stuff" they're dealing with. It took me a long time to realise and appreciate this.

Looking back now, I realise that all the experiences and events in my life have been the making of me. They've defined who I am and made me a more relatable, thoughtful and accomplished human being.

It sounds a bit like a fairy tale, doesn't it? A nice, comfortable beginning in life followed by trials and challenges and then a happy ending... but I feel that my story is more like the "Ugly Duckling", who looked at her reflection one day and realised that she was a "Swan", after all.

6

Mirror! Mirror!

I LOVE to draw parallels from stories and liken them to my own situations. My self-esteem and confidence issues as a teenager and young adult clearly stemmed from the constant stream of insults and name-calling I was subjected to - but the real impact of that was felt when I looked in the mirror.

Words are quite powerful. Once the words "fatso" and "okotombo" had been said to me - and once I'd heard and absorbed them - the job was completed by my mirror. It confirmed exactly what had been said to me.

Why? Because I was looking for it.

Every day, my mirror would tell me I was fat and unattractive. It would disempower me - and I know I'm not alone in this. What's more, I even concluded that I must have been stupid and worthless, too, because people treated me with disrespect - and then I looked in the mirror and did the rest of the job for them by confirming to myself everything they said to me.

I mean, there's no connection between being overweight and being stupid: so, why the leap? Most of us subject ourselves to this self-inflicted abuse because someone else sowed questions and a seed of doubt in our minds. But who are they to tell us who we are? And, worse still, how can we let a mirror - an inanimate object - seal the deal and render us worthless?

When we think about it, it is clear that it's ridiculous.

So here's my take on it:

A mirror is defined as a surface that reflects a clear image. It is an **object**.

A mirror is there for us to check our **appearance** to ensure that we're presentable - nobody wants to go out with their fly down or their skirt tucked into their underwear.

Mirrors can also be helpful for safety purposes; that's why we have them on our cars, motorcycles and bicycles. So: yes, mirrors are useful and necessary!

Do they always give a clear image? I don't think so (if you've ever been in a hall of mirrors at the fairground, you'll know they don't). Some mirrors can make us look long, some can make us look wide, some can make us look squiggly. How, then, can any of us rely on a mirror to tell us the truth?

The day I realised this truth was the day I took my power back from the mirror. I decided that, rather than look at my image in the mirror, I'd prefer to look at myself – into my eyes and soul. I wanted to see **me**! The phrase "can you look yourself in the mirror?" suddenly began to mean something to me.

I wanted to be a "me" that I loved, liked and respected! So, I got to work.

There's a wonderful human being in all of us if we give him, her or them a chance. The more I've worked on the inner me, the more the outer me has evolved into an attractive and beautiful person. I am no longer reliant on - or afraid of - my mirror.

I've learnt that if we focus more on developing ourselves, we can look in our mirrors and see the most beautiful reflection of all.

The first thing I did on my journey of self-discovery and self-acceptance all those years ago was to take a piece of paper and a pen and write down all the good things that I could think of about myself. Things like my personality traits, qualities, abilities, skills, talents and knowledge.

Some of the things I came up with were:

- My genuine and straightforward nature.
- My capacity for kindness and forgiveness.
- My dance moves!

The list grew. Sure, some of them might have been silly and I might have left a lot out (back then, I didn't yet know that I was a good speaker, for example) but they were **all** validating.

I also looked at things I didn't like about myself: it turns out, that list was a short one. Now, that was a revelation! On paper, I didn't **look** like the kind of person that should be disrespected...

The moment I completed that simple exercise, I decided: **no more!**

No more just **surviving. Thriving** was my new aim.

Things didn't change overnight, of course, but I'd now started the work.

Growing and developing myself involved having to step out of my comfort zone on many occasions and face some resistance (mainly from myself...). Mindset is such a powerful thing: I needed a serious change in my mindset. This is still an ongoing process for me as I experience life and reach for greater heights.

I would, therefore, like to share with you what I've learnt from my experiences: how did I get from where I was then to where I am now? I'm going to use a training model I specifically developed for young people - but it can also be applied to any individual of any age at any point in their life. The only thing you need is a desire to **develop confidence, thrive in life and excel in your endeavours**.

It's called "The Thrive Model".

In the next three chapters, I'll focus on the three areas of this training model:

- Confidence.
- Communication.
- Mental health.

THE THRIVE MODEL

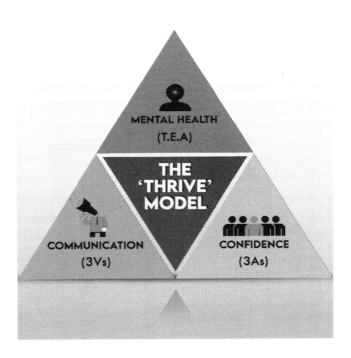

7

Confidence: An Inside Job

How can we be fully self-expressed?

How can we live life on our own terms?

How can we live a life free from the fear of what others think?

The answer: by developing our confidence and self-belief.

Derived from the Latin words *Cum Fides* (with faith), the word "confidence" suggests a sense of self-assurance. It's the feeling of belief that one has in oneself.

Having self-confidence has so many benefits too, besides promoting positive mental health. People who have self-confidence attract others' belief in them, as well, and consequently will progress and do well.

My intention here is not to state the obvious or sell the concept of acquiring or developing self-confidence but to gently reiterate what we already know so that we're clear about what we aim to achieve.

In these three chapters, I will be presenting the text in an enabling and functional way, to foster the creation of an understanding of the concepts - and to share some simple tools with you.

AS A STARTING POINT, let's first address the relationship between self-esteem and self-confidence. Self-confidence can be influenced by self-esteem but, while the two may go hand-in-hand, it's important to understand that they're not the same thing.

Self-esteem is one's view or valuation of oneself which can be based on the opinions or feedback of others. For example, there are many, many successful people who receive positive feedback and applause from others when they've performed well. These people will experience a boost in self-esteem when this happens: but it should not be a foregone conclusion that this means they must be confident people (although they will likely be confident in their field of expertise).

A confident individual is one who maintains a sense of self-belief regardless of the situation they're in.

Simply put:

Self-esteem (high estimation or value of oneself)
Permits others to control your sense of self-worth
and
Self-confidence (self-assurance or self-belief)
*Allows **you** to control your self-worth and life experiences*

Clearly, it's desirable to have both!

UNDERSTANDING CONFIDENCE

Confidence is:

- Faith in your abilities.
- An attitude thing.
- A sense of purpose in life.
- A belief that, within reason, you can do what you **wish, plan** and **expect**.
- Accepting yourself as you are.

Being confident is a major asset in life. It helps you to:

- Deal with uncertainty.
- See challenges as opportunities.
- Take calculated risks.
- Make swift decisions.

Defining confidence for yourself.

To define what confidence means to you, think of a situation in which you felt supremely confident. How did you feel? You might say to yourself:

- I felt valued.
- I felt in control.
- I felt that my achievement had been recognised.
- I felt that I was being listened to and taken seriously.

By analysing what makes you feel good about yourself, you can incorporate more morale-boosting experiences into your life and so maintain your high self-esteem. This will encourage you to step out of your comfort zone, thus building confidence.

Now, let's get to work!

I've laid out two exercises for you to do. Remember that list I created for myself, as my first step on my journey to reclaiming myself? Now it's your turn!

Just like I did, the first thing you'll be doing is creating a list of every single thing you like about yourself. What good and beautiful qualities are you fortunate enough to possess? Put in absolutely everything that comes to mind - including what other people have mentioned to you.

Take your time with this - make sure you can have a comprehensive list. If you get stuck, ask people you know and trust to help you. It can be quite a morale-boosting experience, getting others involved to highlight your qualities, strengths and abilities. So simple, so effective!

The second exercise is a mini journal.

Write something you can recall from your life that you're proud of or for which you received praise. It doesn't have to be anything big. I would recommend writing it in a journal or doing it on a laptop and saving it. It will be an important account to refer to from time to time - especially when you need to step out of your comfort zone or just when you need a reminder that you **are** able.

PERSONAL EXERCISE 1

- Make a list of all the good qualities you possess.
- Make a list of all your skills, talents and gifts.
- Can these skills, talents and gifts be developed and utilised to promote your endeavours? If so, identify which ones.

"Always focus on the things you are good at and never on your failings. Everyone has failings." — Anon.

PERSONAL EXERCISE 2

Write down one thing you've achieved or one thing you've done well:

FINALLY: THE CONFIDENCE BOX

This is where we'll collect and store everything that we're doing to build our confidence. The Confidence Box focuses on four main areas of our lives. If you take these challenges on in your personal life and engage yourself with working on them, your confidence box will grow - and so will your sense of self-belief and self-assurance.

The Confidence Box

Personal development:

- Identify your good qualities.
- Develop your skills.
- Read good books.
- Learn new things.

Health and fitness:

- Look after your mental well-being.
- Have a good diet and exercise regularly.
- Pay attention to your appearance.
- Maintain a good level of hygiene.

Social well-being:

- Develop your communication skills.
- Involve yourself in your community.
- Participate in recreational activities.
- Have good manners - be respectful.

Contribution:

- Help others - family, friends, acquaintances and strangers.
- Give your time to worthy causes.
- Donate to a charity if you're in a position to do so.
- Allow others to contribute to you.

8

Mental Health: Let's Have T.E.A!

THE FIRST THING I'd like to address in this chapter is an understanding of what mental health **is** - we'll also have a brief look at stress management. The objective here is not to gain an in-depth knowledge of mental health but to learn how to manage our personal mental health in a proactive and do-able way.

As in the previous two chapters, this will read more like a simple and brief manual to aid workable application in day-to-day life.

UNDERSTANDING MENTAL HEALTH

The World Health Organisation defines health as:

"A state of complete **physical**, **mental** and **social** wellbeing and not merely the absence of disease and infirmity."

PHYSICAL WELLBEING   MENTAL WELLBEING   SOCIAL WELLBEING

This is what a healthy person looks like - or, to rephrase, this is a 'picture of health'.

Armed with this knowledge, I'm sure we can appreciate that looking after our overall well-being (and not just the physical aspect of our lives) is very important.

A FEW DEFINITIONS

Mental health

The level of our psychological well-being: everyone has mental health.

Positive mental health

"A state of well-being in which every individual realises his or her own potential, can cope with normal stresses of life, can work productively and fruitfully and is able to contribute to his or her community" - (World Health Organisation, 2014).

Mental ill-health

A state of being that affects a person's ability to:

- Work or study.
- Carry out daily activities.
- Engage in satisfying personal relationships.

Mental health issues are a normal part of life and are common - and particularly common are stress-related issues, mild to severe depression and anxiety disorders. This is far from an exhausted list but, for the purposes of developing coping strategies, I'm going to address the issue of stress and resilience.

STRESS

Stress is how the body and brain responds to emotional or physical tension. Stress is something that we all experience: a normal part of our lives. It's not always a bad thing; in fact, a certain level of stress is necessary for us to tune up our brains and improve our performance. Too little stress can lead to boredom and a reduction in performance - but the main area of concern is when an individual faces more stress than they can cope with. This is known as **chronic stress**.

We need to safeguard ourselves against chronic stress because it can:

- Have a serious impact on our physical health.
- Lead to mental health issues.

POSSIBLE STRESS TRIGGERS:

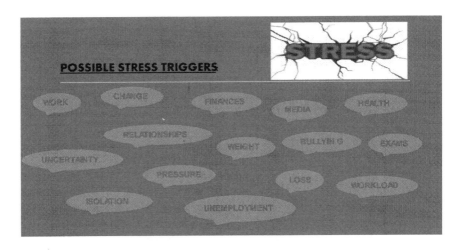

We each need to identify what our triggers or stressors are - managing them then becomes realistic and do-able. Below are three questions I ask myself and use as a managing tool for my stress and anxiety levels before things get too serious for me.

I picked this up during my mental health first aid training course with MIND UK (a course certified by Mental Health First Aid England). The course identified seven questions we can use to deal with triggers - three of those just resonated so well with me and I found them easy to remember. These three questions have served as a powerful coping strategy for me - especially during the pandemic.

I ask myself the following once I've ascertained that I need to address my stress levels:

1. Can anyone **help** me?
2. What are some of my usual **unhelpful** coping strategies?
3. What are some of my **helpful** coping strategies?

These questions help me think and then process what's going on with me - a very useful exercise because it can help me put things into perspective. I'll then look at what I can control or where others can step in to give support or aid.

This enables me to have some control over the situation and gain some perspective.

Control **minimises** uncertainty, while perspective **maximises** hope. That's one powerful recipe for managing mental health!

This is a simple but powerful exercise for managing stress or worries.

At this point, I'd like to propose taking a more proactive approach to managing our mental health - in addition to these three questions. This is where we look after our mental health with the same attitude as our physical health. I call this '**brushing our teeth**'.

Each day, we perform rituals in order to take care of our bodies and fortify ourselves against illness and - so that, even if we were to become ill or injured, our bodies will stand a good chance of recovery. We brush our teeth, wash our bodies, eat, drink, exercise, iron our clothes and cut our hair - and the list goes on. Some of these self-care tasks we do daily and some just regularly; but they've all become routine. They are rituals. What do we have in place for our mental health? Just like we've developed some physical resilience, we must also develop some mental and emotional resilience, too.

Rituals and routines will differ from person to person because we're all unique people with unique circumstances and we all experience unique lives. There are, however, some habits that we can all develop to help build resilience:

- Talk about your worries and concerns - have T.E.A with someone.
- Give yourself a break.
- Create a hassle-free zone – Have some 'Me 'time.
- Have a routine.
- Take care of yourself - body, spirit and sleep.
- Focus on things you can control.
- Help or serve somebody.
- Create a gratitude list.
- Keep a journal.
- Find things to enjoy.
- Control exposure to media when it gets too much.
- Put things into perspective.

This isn't an exhaustive list, as mindfulness can also play a very crucial part in switching off from a stressful environment or mental state, thus enabling being present in a calm moment. For instance:

- I use puzzles and colouring books to chill myself out.
- Some people grow and look after plants.

- Reading is also another highly effective mindfulness tool.
- Walking and taking in the environment or nature is a positive mindfulness activity.
- Meditating is great for mindfulness and managing anxiety.
- Making our beds when we get up in the morning is a simple but effective action to get our minds focused for a positive day ahead.

These are only a few suggestions and I've selected these in particular because they're my personal favourites. Please bear in mind that I'm not suggesting we do all of them: we must all choose or find whatever works best for ourselves.

NOW LET'S HAVE T.E.A!

The top tip for developing resilience or for recovering from mental ill-health is to talk about our worries and issues.

Talking about our issues and concerns and stamping out stigma is at the heart of creating a space in our communities where mental health is recognised and accepted as normal.

It's become evident to me that **tea** is somewhat of a problem solver for us in England - or so it seems. Tea is a soothing balm in times of difficulty or distress, and making someone **a nice cup of tea** provides an opportunity to give comfort or lend a listening ear. Tea has often been described as the perfect tonic in a crisis: I call it a soothing balm for pain.

Let's Have T.E.A! is a training session I developed to equip people to become more comfortable and open around the subject of their mental health. Most of us are aware that talking about our mental health is crucial to recovery and contributes to normalising it in our communities - and, yet, when it comes down to it, we still hold back and hesitate to disclose what exactly is going on with us until it becomes a serious issue.

The **Let's Have T.E.A!** session breaks down the conversation around disclosure into three areas:

1. **T**alking about 'it'.
2. **E**xpressing emotion.
3. **A**ccepting help and support.

For each of these three aspects of T.E.A, though there may be perceived **obstacles,** there are **solutions** to overcome them. A powerful starting point is to start talking to trusted ones about our worries, concerns and issues.

My vision is to live in a society where mental health is seen in the same light as physical health. So...**Let's Start Having T.E.A!**

9

Communication: An Outside Job

MOVING FORWARD from the conversations about confidence and mental health, it's important to have effective communication skills - they can contribute hugely to our Confidence Box. There are so many benefits to having good communication skills! Benefits like:

- Helping to foster trust with others.
- Enabling a message to be conveyed clearly.
- Enhancing confidence.
- Improving productivity.
- Enhancing social interaction.
- Talking about important issues, like mental health.
- Strengthening personal relationships.

And, on the topic of personal relationships, I've found that developing my communication skills *(especially when jumping in at the deep end and joining a speakers' club many years ago!)* has enhanced my experience of life. I enjoy being with people and I'm very comfortable meeting new people, which was something I struggled with when I was a teenager.

I remember the first time I had to give a speech in public - it was a terrifying and nerve-racking experience, and I didn't think that I would survive. I survived and it was 'ok', but with time and with a positive mindset I got better. Now, I'm able to use the skills I've developed over the years to express myself clearly in a way that creates understanding and removes any possibility of contention or resentment. I'm a better listener and I've learnt not to interrupt others but, instead, to hear them out before having my say. I'm now more confident in unfamiliar situations and environments like interviews and networking events and I'll happily introduce myself to strangers at social gatherings or in a queue at a supermarket without worrying about rejection or what they might think about me. I even took off to India in 2018 to contribute to a community where I didn't know anyone - and, as a result, gained friends and family who are now very important parts of my life. I'm now living a life where I can be my authentic self and where people respond positively to me - **and I am loving it!**

I would, therefore, like to share with you some tools that have helped me as a communicator.

One very effective way to develop our communication skills is to learn how to speak to groups of people: public speaking! A concept absolutely dreaded by most people (myself included, at one point!). It's one of the best ways to step out of our comfort zones, improve our communication skills and develop confidence.

I know that public speaking and presenting is not for everyone - but everyone can learn a tip or two from these techniques to enhance their communication skills and make them more effective in getting a thought, an idea or a message across. So, please bear with me if you fall into the category of those who may think that these tools or tips may not be for you - because, one day, you may need to attend an interview, make a pitch for your business, go to a networking event, make small talk at a social gathering or ask someone out on a date. (*Of course, I've had the latter down since I was six, if you recall...!*)

I've worked in association with Speakers Trust, a charity that delivers public speaking training to young people, since 2005 and to date I've now delivered over 1,000 workshops to over 50,000 young people who've gone on to become confident communicators - so, I can tell you that the tips and tools in this chapter have been tried and tested.

Here, I'll be sharing some tips and tools with you on how to deliver a speech if you need to. I'll then highlight how some of these tools and tips can be transferred into other areas of our lives.

To simplify this, I'll break down the content into a workable document so you can quickly and easily understand what's required.

When presenting, it's important to understand the three elements of engaging an audience or your listeners:

- VISUAL - **What they see** - Expressions and appearance.
- VOCAL - **What they hear** - Sound.
- VERBAL - **What they hear** - Words.

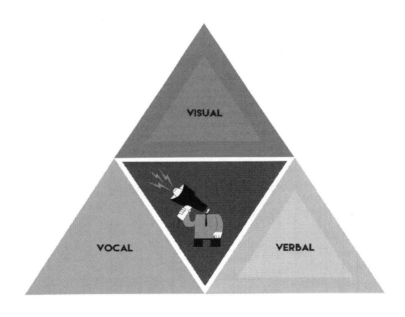

OVERCOMING NERVES

Nerves are natural.

They'll never go away completely - but you can use tips and techniques to help you conquer them.

Nerves help you give your best when you're speaking publicly: try some of the following tips to help you feel more in control.

1. Know your material and be prepared.

Have short notes/words on a sheet of paper **or** small pieces of card. Know your key message.

2. Practise.

In front of a mirror, at home, in a car, to your friends and colleagues. Hear yourself speak - you can always tape yourself. Confidence and certainty come from practice.

3. Remember to breathe.

Take some deep breaths before you speak. This will both ease any tension you have and help you project your voice. Breathe and stretch!

4. Keep your opening and conclusion short and simple. Memorise them.

This makes you appear confident and authoritative, and you then have eye contact with your audience - which gets them to listen to you.

. . .

5. Understand that your audience wants you to succeed.

They're on your side! They can't see the butterflies in your tummy, your sweaty palms or your shaking knees. They're only listening to what you have to say!

6. Imagine yourself speaking to a large audience.

Picture the room, see the people, hear the applause. Visualise yourself being successful.

7. Plan.

Remember that proper planning creates a good performance: **prior preparation prevents poor performance.** The 5 'P's

8. Never apologise.

The audience will never know if you leave out half your talk or take things in a different order. Simply use the power of the pause and continue.

9. Stage management and presence.

Your speech should be sandwiched between 4 'W's.

1. *Walk* on to the stage confidently.
2. *Wait* for two seconds before speaking.
3. *Wait* two seconds after your speech to allow the message to sink in, then:
4. *Walk* confidently off the stage.

10. **Take every opportunity to speak.**

Remember that public speaking is a skill, like learning to drive a car. Practice and experience always work best.

TO SUMMARIZE

Preparation and practise - **The 5 Ps**
(PRIOR PREPARATION PREVENTS POOR PERFORMANCE)

Manage composure - **The 4 Ws**
(WALK - WAIT - WAIT – WALK)

Your **audience** wants **you** to **succeed.**
(THEY'RE JUST WAITING FOR YOU TO SPEAK)

VOCAL IMPACT - THE 3Ps!

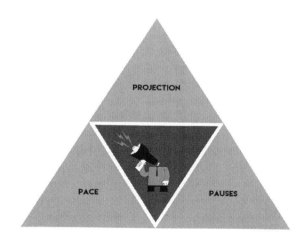

The three 'Powerful Ps' Explained:

- **Project** so that your voice has power and your audience can hear you.

- **Pace** yourself well, so that you don't rush your speech - this results in better delivery.

- **Pause** for impact and to give your audience time to think and take it all in.

TOP 10 TIPS FOR SPEAKING IN PUBLIC

1. Be your authentic self:

This is **your** chance to speak up - **your** views, **your** stories, what **you** think should be done. It's not a performance: it's an opportunity to engage with your listeners.

2. Eye contact:

Making regular eye contact with individual members of your audience will ensure you maintain their interest. This is also a powerful emotional tool to ensure a connection. Spread your focus: don't pick just one or two people with whom to make eye contact.

3. Structure your talk:

A clear outline or framework will assist you in remembering what you want to say and will assist your audience in understanding your message. Make sure it has a clear **introduction** (opening), **key message** (body) and **conclusion** (end):

- **Introduction** - A strong start really helps you to hook the audience. Issue a challenge, make a joke, give a quote or ask a question.

- **Key Message** - A useful guideline is to have three key points to your talk. What can you include to maintain the attention of the emotional, logical and factual listener?
- **Conclusion** - Finish confidently and with conviction - a call to action, a challenge, a strong summary or a question. Your audience will remember best what they hear last.

4. Keep it simple:

Tailor your speech to your audience. Communication is about connecting and sharing.

5. Pause:

In speaking, the power of silence can greatly add to the impact of your delivery and message. Taking a breath is much more effective than "um" or "er".

6. Speak from the heart and with enthusiasm:

Show your passion. Be excited about your message, bring it alive and you will take your audience with you. Be honest, genuine and sincere.

7. Use your voice and your body:

Good posture, gestures, facial expressions and vocal variety (i.e. pitch, **pace**, pauses and volume) enhance your performance.

8. Know your time limit and don't overrun:

Deliver your talk/make your point(s) - and then sit down. Keeping to time communicates a certain level of professionalism and respect for your audience.

9. Project your voice

Project your voice to the back of the room so that your audience can hear you easily. This also enhances your performance by giving the impression of a powerful speaker.

10. Practice! Again the 5 Ps.

Try out your speech in front of friends, family, in your head and even in front of a mirror at home. Get feedback. Remember that experience is everything - **always say "yes!"** to a speaking opportunity.

STRUCTURING A SPEECH

Structuring a speech is like a three-course meal:

- Starter (**opening or introduction**) - wet their appetites, so they want more.

- Main course (**main body or message**) - fill them up with three key points.

- Dessert (**conclusion or end**) - finish off with a short and sweet wrap-up.

"Food is to the body what words are to the mind."- *Ore Ogungbayi*

That's a phrase of mine that I've become fairly well-known for using, and often! Whenever you're speaking to an audience, assume that you're feeding them your information or content - gently feeding, not shoving it down their throats.

TEMPLATE OF THE STRUCTURE

Opening (15%) - *Do they want to hear more?*

Facts. Rhetorical question. Quote. Personal story. Humour. Time - Place - Incident. Set the scene and outline early .

Body (75%) - *Your main message in three key points.*

Are you informing or inspiring, persuading or motivating? Choose an approach: chronological sequence / comparisons / contrasts / problem / solution / cause / effect. Support each point with evidence, explanation or endorsement (who, what, why, when, where). Use a short summary as a transition between points. Avoid clichés!

Conclusion (10%) - *A memorable thought!*

Memorise it and don't add any new points - this is a summary of the main points, calling back to your opening.

Include a call to action - offer alternative solutions, issue a challenge or leave them with a question.

TOOLS & TIPS FOR OTHER SITUATIONS

Now, let's have a look at how some of these tools can be helpful in all sorts of other situations - not just public speaking:

The three 'V's.

What we say (**verbal**), how we sound (**vocal**) and how we seem (**visual**) can impact how we come across to other people - especially when they're meeting us for the first time.

"First impressions count!" - we've all heard that from time to time. Yet, I ask myself if this is a fair assessment of any individual. What if someone catches me on a bad day? They clearly won't get the best of me but - fair or not - a first impression may be the only chance we get. It, therefore, stands to reason that we need to put our best foot forward as far as communication skills are concerned when meeting people for the first time, be it formal or informal.

Let's take an interview for example. Within the three 'V's, we have a host of tools to help us make a great impression. I'll make a list, just for fun, and then I'll expect you to apply and adapt this list to other situations going forward.

Here's my list:

• You arrive at an interview (early) and you make yourself known to the receptionist. You make **eye contact** and **smile**.

• While waiting to be called in, you go over the things you've prepared to say - the 5 'P's (**prior preparation prevents poor performance**).

• When you're called in, you **walk** in **confidently** and greet the interviewer or panel with a **clear** and **well-projected** voice and you make **eye contact**. They get the impression that you're confident.

• On entering the room, you sit up with good **posture** and use effective **body language**. This will put everyone (including yourself) at ease.

• If there's more than one person (a panel), you make **eye contact** with each one of them when answering a question, even if only one person has asked you the question. You don't just focus on the questioner.

• You listen to the questions and **pause** briefly for thought before responding. If necessary, you may even ask for clarification if the question is not clear. **You never panic!**

• You speak **clearly** and at a good **pace** when answering a question. By doing this, you now have more control than you would have done otherwise and you don't run the risk of stuttering.

• You **know** your stuff and believe in yourself.

• When asked to talk about yourself, you've come **prepared** with a **well-structured** (three-course meal) mini-speech in your head.

Imagine that this is you in different situations drawing upon these skills. You will be impressive! So, as you can see, public speaking skills are as useful off stage as on.

10

A Dozen Lessons

I'VE WRITTEN this book during an incredibly challenging time in the world: the COVID-19 pandemic.

It's been a time when most people have had to take stock of their lives and decide what's important to them – and, in some cases, give themselves a second chance at life and, hopefully, do better. I've been one of those people, too. One of the things I discovered is that writing my story with the purpose of sharing, inspiring and uplifting people is very important to me.

My biological mother, Victoria, who is so dear to me, has been very encouraging, as have my two daughters, Feyi and Feto. They feel very strongly about the impact my story might have on the lives of others. I thank them!

I'd like to share 12 lessons I've learnt from my experiences in life:

Lesson 1

After reflecting on my past and current experiences, it's clear to me that the first lesson I learnt is to be **grateful** and **show appreciation**.

Gratitude and appreciation for my experiences, for the loved ones in my life, for what others do for me (no matter how small) and for any situation I may find myself in. Gratitude and appreciation are so important: because, you know what? Things could always be worse.

Lesson 2

I've learnt that I am responsible for my attitude and how I treat others.

I have the power to choose to be positive, kind and honest regardless of the situation. How I behave in the most challenging of situations will show me and the world who I really am.

Lesson 3

I've learnt that no situation is permanent. Hard times come and go - good times come and go.

Life was designed that way and this is how we grow as individuals and achieve our full potential. I've fought many battles (and won quite a few of them!) so I reckon I'm going to win the war.

Lesson 4

I've learnt that I am not alone.

There are others with challenges, difficulties and trials just like mine and there's always a way to find support and acceptance. We all belong somewhere! Somewhere where we're loved and accepted for who we are. Somewhere we find peace and enjoy a sense of self-worth.

Lesson 5

I've learnt that not everyone will like me.

It doesn't matter how lovely and wonderful I try to be, I will not please everyone. **This has been my hardest and most painful lesson.** It's been exhausting trying to be everyone's 'cup of tea'. I want to be liked and accepted by everyone but, through the experiences I've had, I realise that, besides God, the only person whose acceptance and validation I should seek is... **Ore's.**

I have now accepted myself for everything I am - and everything I'm not.

Lesson 6

I've learnt that everyone needs to be proactive with their mental health.

We all have our daily and regular rituals that we perform to safeguard our physical wellbeing, which have become routine for us - things we do without thinking. We need to develop the same approach to our mental health.

Lesson 7

I've learnt that every person I meet is superior to me in some way.

This means that, regardless of their circumstances, every individual I come into contact with will possess a talent, skill, ability or quality that I can learn or benefit from. I should, therefore, never let arrogance get in the way of respecting another human being.

Lesson 8

I've learnt never to be afraid to ask for help or support. No person is an island!

Especially where my mental health is concerned, I've adopted a more open approach to expressing myself and my concerns to others. There's no shame or weakness in asking for and accepting help. In fact, it takes strength to ask!

Lesson 9

I've learnt that any one of us can achieve our goals.

Goals require a vision and effort. If you can visualise it, it is achievable. If you can put the effort in, it will be achieved. I have a poster on my bathroom wall that reads:

"**Imagine** with all your mind - **Believe** with all your Heart - **Achieve** with all your might"

These are the principles I've been applying as I've moved forward on my journey.

Lesson 10

I've learnt that I am a **strong woman**!

This is a biggie for me. During those years I refer to as 'my years of abuse', I never knew who I was or of what I was capable. Yet, it was those years that created the foundation for me to springboard myself from. Those years have taught me that strength cannot be developed from ease but from resistance (just ask anyone who works out at a gym!).

Lesson 11

I've learnt that to fully enjoy what the world and life have to offer I must embrace everyone, appreciate all cultures and respect every religion.

I've learnt to respect the individual choice to believe in or not to believe in something. I believe in worshipping God according to the dictates of my own conscience and that everyone should have the same privilege – let them worship how, where or what they may – or not. I now see myself as the possibility of love, freedom and power in the world and I do my best to anchor myself with these three ways of being.

Lesson 12

I've learnt through personal experience that **love knows no colour!**

You've read my story and I think it's evident from my account that **love is love**. I am grateful that I had the opportunity to have two sets of parents from different cultures who loved me and were prepared to do anything to keep me. In my world, there's no room for 'them and us'. In my world, there's only room for '**US**'.

OVERALL LESSON:

We're not just on this journey of life to survive: we're on it to THRIVE!

Some Thoughts from the Heart

My mentor, Richie Dayo Johnson (RDJ), (who fondly called me "Ms Lou" and who sadly passed away before I could finish this book) taught me many invaluable lessons. I'd like to leave three of these thoughts with you:

1. **Remember: every man or woman you meet is superior to you in some way.** This is not suggesting that we are not capable - rather, it is a statement to remind us not to let our capabilities make us arrogant. I mentioned this in the previous chapter as one of the 12 lessons that I have learnt, and I mention it again because "Constant repetition carries conviction" – *Robert Collier.*
2. **To be a great leader, you need to find others to whom you can show the way - so that they can become greater than you.** I've always loved this concept because we keep ourselves small when we're afraid of the accomplishments of others.
3. **Never say "no" to an opportunity that comes your way just because you feel inadequate.** Even if you don't know everything there is to know about the task, there will always

be someone else who does and you can ask them for their insight and support.

I've been extremely fortunate to have experienced myriad things that have helped to shape me as a person and enrich my life in general. I've never been one for theme parks and you'll never catch me on a ride that's anywhere near thrilling - yet, my life has been one big roller coaster ride! At a theme park, I always play the role of spectator, watching and enjoying others having a wonderful time while I stand by the wayside - but I've always been front-and-centre on the ride of life, participating, and with the ups and downs and the twists and turns I've ended up having the experience of **my life**.

I've gone **from hopeless to hopeful**: I'm no longer just surviving - I am **thriving**!

Fear, low self-esteem, feelings of inadequacy, not fitting in, rejection and many more things that get in the way of living life fully have plagued me at some point in my life. Now, though, after years of experience, I realise that they were all there for me to conquer so that I could be the **me** who was born to be great.

We were all born to become the greatest versions of ourselves, no matter our circumstances - but sadly the unpleasantries and hardships of life can overpower us into submission and mean that we don't quite make it.

Everyone has a story to tell. What's yours? How has it impacted you and others?

Does your story hold you back or propel you forward?

Do others get to tell you your worth or do you decide?

What legacy would you like to build and leave behind?

A huge proportion of my young life was spent feeling inferior and less deserving compared to others - but, today, I can say with complete honesty: "I **LIKE ME**".

Printed in Great Britain
by Amazon